My Legal Sicilian Immigrants

By

Jo Del Tufo

My Legal Sicilian Immigrants

Written by Jo (Testa) Del Tufo
Copyright 2015 Jo Del Tufo

Janjo Publishing
A division of Janjo LLC
www.Janjo.biz
mail@Janjo.biz

First Edition

All rights reserved. No part of this book may be used or reproduced in any manner whatsoever without prior written permission of the author/publisher, except in the case of brief quotations embodied in reviews.

ISBN number 978-1-943116-01-0

I dedicate this book to my children, nieces and nephews.

Table of Contents

Introduction

Prologue

Chapter One: Grampa

Chapter Two: Gramma

Chapter Three: Gertrude

Chapter Four: Catherine

Chapter Five: Teddy

Chapter Six: Helen

Chapter Seven: Norma

Chapter Eight: Josephine

Chapter Nine: Mike

Chapter Ten: Albert

Additional photos

Title Page

Introduction

Josephine Del Tufo grew up in Bloomfield, New Jersey, in a home with two brothers and four sisters. Her mother and father emigrated from Italy in 1908, and family controversies were part of her life throughout adulthood. Some controversies ended peacefully and some ended in pain and sorrow. Josephine tells a short family story in her book "My Legal Sicilian Immigrants" and sends love to her family.

The Testa Family of Bloomfied, New Jersey 1945.

Top row from left are Mike, Catherine, Teddy, Angelina, Michele and Josephine.

Bottom row from left are Helen, Gertrude and Norma

Prologue

MY LEGAL SICILIAN IMMIGRANTS
(I dedicate this story to my children, nieces and nephews.)
Questo Storia e Avere L'ultimo Parola Compreso Mia Opinione
(This story is to "have the last word" including my opinions)

It was the year 1908. Families left their Sicilian villages behind to board huge ships and cross the great Atlantic Ocean to live out the American dream. Two of those families from separate villages took to the seas during that time of heavy European immigration into the United States. It is not certain these two families were on the same ship, but they both arrived in the same year. Michele Testa from the town of Cerami and Angelina Dispenziere from the town of Galgliano were two of those arrivals.

They landed on Ellis Island in New York, which was the gateway center for millions of immigrants to America. Later in life, they both recalled how difficult it was for Americans to understand them when asked their names, ages and other pertinent information. No one brought along birth certificates to assist with processing.

It was 100 percent verbal; therefore, names were often misspelled. Michele (Michael spelled in Italian) was 14 years old and Angelina was 8 at the time of their arrivals. Both families joined respective relatives living in Montclair, New Jersey and they lived fairly close to one another. They settled in a small area then considered their own "Little Italy."

Many years later, Michele and Angelina met at the Oakes Mill Textile Factory in Bloomfield, New Jersey. It was there they worked and fell in love. They married September of 1921 at Our Lady of Mount Carmel Catholic Church on Pine Street in Montclair. This church still exists, and this is how my Testa family began.

Now as I write this story about each member of my family, I do so with words of love, mostly facts and some of my opinions.

Gramma and Grandpa (Angelina and Michele) on their wedding day in 1920.

Chapter One: Grampa

Over the years, our family experienced many controversies, but they all worked themselves out. I will start with my Moma and PaPa as we called them and better known to the grandchildren as Gramma and Grampa Testa.

Grampa attended school in Sicily until leaving the country but had no schooling at all in America. Gramma had two years of education in Sicily and none at all in the U.S. It was not mandatory in that era for immigrants to attend school; therefore, it was easier simply to not go to school. Grampa, however, was a very brilliant man. He spoke Italian and broken English.

He began married life with a desire for independence and a longing to start his own business. With a pick and a shovel, he dug ditches in order to install home furnaces. It was such very hard work.

He possessed a split personality. He was so nice sometimes and had many friends who loved him. However, there were other times he was nasty, mean and sometimes very abusive, in particular to Aunt Helen and to Uncle Teddy. That was disturbing and painful for me.

Aside from his backbreaking occupation, his absolutely greatest accomplishment in his life was his gift for producing the best vegetable garden in all of New Jersey. He grew every vegetable imaginable, but best of all were his tomatoes. (They were the very best on the East Coast.) People would come from all over to our front yard to buy bags of tomatoes.

The only problem with this wonderful talent was when August 15 of each year came around and I would get a phone call from Gamma. "You can come over tomorrow, the tomatoes are ready," she would say. There were bushels of them. That meant washing, cutting, cooking, straining and jarring them for her wonderful "GRAVY," as we all knew it to be.

This was a big pain in the backside for all of us girls who were involved in this task. I worked at it more than any one of my sisters because I lived so close and I was always available. Every year we "put up" approximately 250 quart jars of tomatoes. It was a lot of work, but really worth the effort.

Grampa died of esophageal cancer in the East Orange Veteran's Hospital on January 6, 1967. He was 73 years old.

Grampa (Michele) with Gramma (Angelina)

Chapter Two: Gramma

Gramma; may God bless her. She worked very hard all her life. She had very little education and spoke both Italian (broken) and good English, even though she would botch words up in a very cute and funny way. When she referred to the English language she would always say, "I will speak American."

I remember her washing clothes by hand with a washboard in the kitchen sink and hanging laundry out on a clothesline to dry. In the cold winter months, the clothes froze on the line, making the drying time even longer. She then ironed everything, even sheets and pillowcases.

She made her own pasta and bread, and she cooked a terrific meal for her family every night. She baked a cookie called "Cavadeda," which looked similar to a ladyfinger. She stored them in a big barrel in the front room closet. All you grandchildren knew right where they were, and you frequently raided that closet.

In Gramma's spare time, she sewed on a treadle machine and made all our clothes, including underwear. With all this, she never complained. She was the sweetest mother a person could ever have or want.

Gamma gave birth to nine children. Her second child, Joseph, died from diphtheria at 7 month of age. It was an epidemic at that time. The second child to pass away was my little brother Albert, which was a sad and tragic story. He was 6 and I was 11.

Before Albert was born, Gramma tried to abort him on her own as she really did not want or need another child. The abortion failed and at birth, Albert needed to have a kidney removed. There was not treatment or transplants for this problem in those times. Doctors told Gramma and Grampa that he would have a very short life because he could not live on one kidney for very long. You cannot imagine how they spoiled him. He was a complete brat, but we loved him anyway and missed him for a long time after he passed.

There is one last mention to Gramma's life. Her grandmother was an illegitimate child to a French Lieutenant way back when. There may be some French blood in all of us. Ha!

Gramma was diabetic and had heart disease. She died of a massive heart attack on June 25, 1971, just one month short of her 71st birthday.

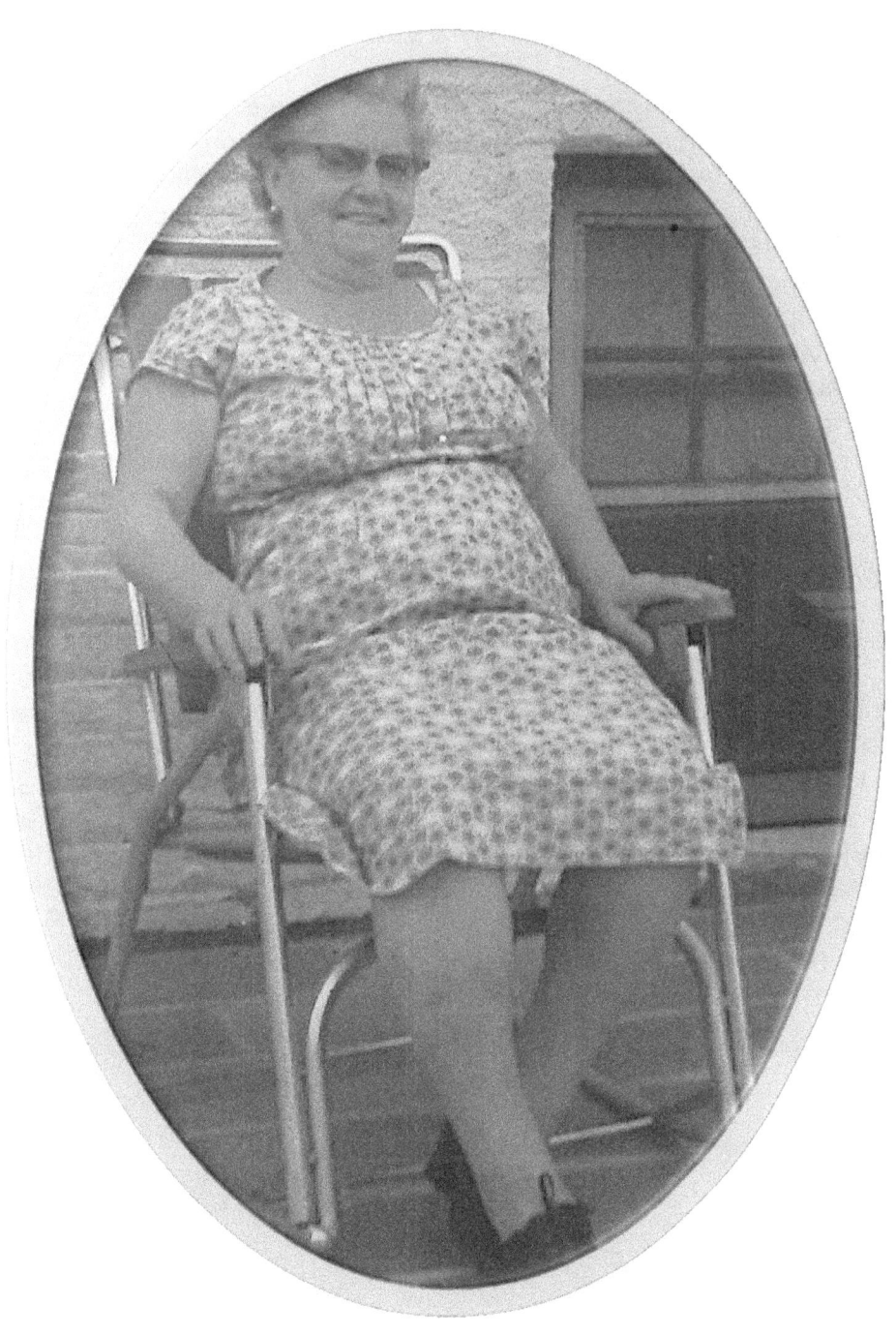

Gramma (Angelina) loved sitting out in her chair

Chapter Three: Gertrude

The first-born child was Gaetana (better known to us as Gertrude) born on August 5, 1922. Grampa's siblings all named their first-born girls after their mother, Gaetana. They never correctly enunciated the "T" and called their daughters Dona instead of Tana. Both Gramma and Grampa called their baby "Dona."

As I understand it, one of Dona's teachers told her that she would call her Gertrude, as it was more American and easier to pronounce. We are not certain if her name was ever legally changed. Gramma adapted to her new name, but Grampa called her Dona all his life.

Gertrude was born with beautiful curly blonde hair and blue eyes. Fast forward, she became an acting mother to her siblings because she was the oldest and Gramma was very busy with her life. This was custom in many Italian families where there were several children.

Of course, Gramma needed help but this took an emotional toll on Aunt Gertrude because we all resented her for the authority she had over us. After all, she was only our sister. However, it did not take away our love for her. As children, we all had happy days with her when she would play games with us or read to us. I still remember Gertrude baking the very first cake we ever tasted.

Gertrude married Richard Scott and was the first one in the family to relocate to another state. She moved to Sudbury, Massachusetts with her husband and gave birth to three children, David, Lindsay and Melissa. Gertrude had diabetes and heart disease. She died after a stroke in October of 1990. She was 68 years old.

Next was Joseph, who died as a baby and died before most of us were born so we never saw or knew him.

Gertrude Testa Scott

Chapter Four: Catherine

Now here comes Catherine, born February 29, 1924. A leap year baby named after Grandma's mother, who celebrated her birthday the first day of March. As in the case with Grampa, every one of Gramma's siblings named a daughter Catherine. The custom was to name the first daughter after the mother and the first son after the father, though this was not the exact case in this situation.

Speaking for myself, I grew up feeling as if she were my only sibling. I always wanted to be with her, even though she was seven years older. It was as if she was my own personal babysitter. I loved being with her. When I made my confirmation, she was my sponsor. When I married Albert (Al) Del Tufo, I asked her to be my Maid of Honor. Moreover, when my first child (Albert) was born, she became his Godmother. We were so very close and such great friends.

Catherine was very generous with my children and me, as well as with all her nieces and nephews. She did not have children of her own, but two miscarriages. Her story is a very long one, which everyone knows and is too long to tell. All I will say is that with all the lifelong love I had for her, our relationship ended very sadly. For me it was a disaster.

Catherine became diabetic very late in her life. She developed kidney disease and was on dialysis for several years. Catherine died May 5, 2008 She was 84 years old.

Catherine Testa Laratta

Chapter Five: Teddy

Next was Theodore, better known as Uncle Teddy, who was born September 30, 1926. As children, we always called him Theodore, pronounced as "Thedoor." He hated his name so he took on the name "Teddy" while growing up in school.

Teddy had many problems growing up. He was involved in quite a bit of mischief and because of it severely abused by Grampa. One time while playing baseball outside the house he hit and broke a neighbor's window.

The neighbor brought the broken glass to Grampa to show him what his son had done. The man left and Grampa put the glass on a bench, forcing Uncle Teddy sit on it for a long while as punishment. This was just one of the many disciplinary actions Grampa took with him.

During one of the awful beatings he took from Grampa, I went into a closet, sat on the floor and cried my eyes out. I absolutely hated those days. Teddy grew up to be the hardest working person I ever knew. At age 17, he quit school to join the Navy (Seabees). After arriving home from his tour of duty, Bloomfield High school presented him with a diploma. His grades in school were always excellent. I never saw him do homework, ever. From there he never missed a day's work in his short life.

Teddy married local girl Jackie Benora in 1948. They had one child named Patti Ann. They divorced after two years of marriage. We really did not get to know little Patti Ann. Her mom moved to Newburg, New York and actually kept her from seeing her father and his siblings.

Much later in life, Al and I were in New Jersey visiting our families. Uncle Teddy invited us to his house for Sunday night dinner. It was 1986. When we arrived his wife Joan told me he was not feeling well and was very concerned. I sat with him and questioned him about his symptoms.

I begged him to see a doctor and wanted him to visit the emergency room. He was in bad shape but refused to go. "What will a doctor tell me," he said. "He will tell me to stop working and then put me into the hospital. I can't do that, I have too much work to do and I need the money." I begged him at least to go see a doctor the next day. This went on all evening until about 8 p.m. when he said he wanted to go to bed. He kissed me goodbye and went to sleep.

He got up the following morning at 5 a.m. and went to work for a contractor. He was on his backhoe digging out a foundation for a house. After a couple of hours, he told the men he was working with he needed a rest and was going into his truck. He put his head down on the steering wheel and never woke up. He died of a massive heart attack right there.

I would just like to add something to his life story. Even after the lifelong abuse he received from his father, he supported Gramma and Grampa until they both passed away, despite the fact Grampa did not talk to him for the last 15 years of his life. This was all so sad.

Teddy died on July 28, 1986. He was only 59 years old.

Teddy Testa

Chapter Six: Helen

Helen was born next, on October 7, 1927, with beautiful black hair and blue eyes. Generally, she was very charming, outgoing and personable. She loved being with all her friends.

When we were growing up, we lived in our two-bedroom house on Baldwin Place. Gramma and Grampa occupied one bedroom and the girls shared two beds in the other bedroom. Gertrude and Catherine slept in one bed, and Helen, Norma and I slept in the other. Kind of crowded but we did not know any better.

We actually never knew we were poor, which was a good thing. Where did Teddy and Sonny (Mike) sleep? They slept on a folding bed in the dining room. No one really had any privacy except our parents.

Helen was very independent and did what she wanted despite house rules. She always wanted to be with her friends and she had many. Grampa punished her on a number of occasions for getting home late from school and nearly missing dinner. Grampa handed out severe punishments to her after warning her many times. I will say he was not very nice and his treatment toward her was emotional for me.

Helen married Nick Celfo and had two daughters, Dona and Elena. Helen was diabetic, which caused her many problems. She and Nick retired to North Carolina looking forward to a peaceful and restful retirement, but instead she was ill most of the time. This was very sad. Helen died on June 29, 1996 at the age of 69.

Helen Testa Celfo

Chapter Seven: Norma

Norma was born December 31, 1928. She was 14 months older than I was.

Norma was independent and always wanted it her way or no way. We got along well even though she kept her distance from all of us as children. The irony of this, however, is when we went to bed.

With three of us in one bed, it was quite crowded. Norma never showed affection, but she and I wound up with our legs crossed over each other and our arms around each other after we fell asleep. That is how we slept every night, all night.

The three of us use to organize musical parties like amateur hour, dancing and singing on the bed before we went to sleep. Grampa would yell from the kitchen. "Shut up and go to sleep." We were having fun, so naturally we did not listen.

Often he would come into our room, starting with Helen, and whip her until she cried. Then he would whip Norma, though Norma would never cry … and I mean never. Because she would not cry, she was hit some more. By the time he got to me, I was crying hysterically. So I was not whipped. After he left, you could hear Norma sobbing quietly. She would not give anyone the satisfaction of knowing she was crying. She was stubborn.

When Norma graduated High School, she wanted to go to college. Her grades were fantastic but Grampa told her that she had a choice. "Go to college or stay with your boyfriend." Well we all know the choice she made. She chose to continue dating Uncle Doc (as we all knew him).

When her children were young, she let them do anything they wanted, even if they misbehaved in public. She would not give anyone the satisfaction of seeing her spanking her children. When she got them home, she made up for it.

She married Michael DiOrio and had five children, Kathy, Michael, Lori, Johnny and Gary. She was also diabetic with heart problems. Norma died at age 62 after open-heart surgery.

Norma Testa DiOrio

Chapter Eight: Josephine

Next in line was Josephine. I was third from the last child and I was born on St. Joseph's Day March 19, 1931. This is how I got my name.

My life was hard growing up because I was scared to death of Grampa, probably because of how he disciplined those before me. He never spanked me. I guess because I was afraid to do anything wrong, or I was already crying. He forced me to be a goody two shoes.

He used to read the Italian newspaper to Gramma at the dinner table and that meant we all had to be completely silent. There was a time I was giggling at something and he threw a loaf of bread across the table and knocked out my front tooth. It was probably loose anyway but it left a very bad impression on me.

I was very young when Uncle Al and I started dating. Even before we were dating, he would come to our house pretending to play with Uncle Mike. There were times when Aunt Gertrude would want him to leave and she would say, "You better go home, Albert, I hear your mother calling you." He lived two blocks around the corner. I married Albert Del Tufo, and we have three children, Albert, Janet and Jodi. My children mean the world to me. They are wonderful and I feel so very blessed.

Near the end of Grampa's life, he gave me his car to drive Gramma and him sometimes to and from the hospital. We lived close to Gramma and Grampa in Bloomfield and spent lots of time together. Gramma came to our house every Friday night for me to set her hair. This of course ended when we moved to Arizona.

Just to let you all know May 24, 2015 is officially the day I am oldest living member of my Testa family. I take a lot of pride in this fact. I will say…. It has been a long ride.

Josephine Testa Del Tufo

Chapter Nine: Mike

After me came Mike, known to us throughout our lives as Sonny.

Here we see an example of how birth papers got misconstrued. Gramma and Grampa wanted his name to be Armand. With the language barrier and mispronunciations, his birth certificate read Herman. He grew up with a non-Italian, awful name until just before he went into the service. He legally changed it to Michael. Of course, we all hated the name Herman so we called him Sonny. He was Sonny to us though he would introduce himself as Mike or Uncle Mike. That stuck.

Mike was temperamental, loved attention and gave lots of love to everyone. He felt neglected growing up. He was the baby and the last in line. Mike had a strong desire to be a professional baseball player. There again Grampa discouraged him because he said baseball was not a real job, and therefore did not support his dream. This was sad. Bloomfield High School, however, recognized and honored him by inducting him into the Bloomfield Hall of Fame for Baseball.

Our little families grew up together and were extremely close. We did a lot of visiting and partying amongst ourselves. Mike had a deep love for his kids, which was very nice, but he expressed to me many times that he loved his kids more than we loved ours because we did not openly show affection like kissing and hugging them constantly. Oh well, that was Mike.

There was a controversy going on in the family later in life, which caused Mike to stop speaking to me. The very sad outcome of all of that was when he asked me not to and then thanked me for not coming to see him before he died. That event hurt, and it is too long of a story to include in this book about the Testa Family.

Mike died December 2004. He was also diabetic and had heart problems. He died from Liver Cancer at age 72.

Mike Testa

Chapter Ten: Albert

Lastly, there was my baby brother Albert. I am not sure of his birth date but he was born March of 1938. All I can say is he was the cutest, but brattiest kid alive. That is how I remember him, and we all missed him when he died in September of 1944.

He was in the first grade in Fairview School in Bloomfield when he died. Gramma could never afford to buy our school pictures, so consequently we never had any. However, when Albert died the principal and his teacher came to our house out of sympathy and presented us with his school pictures. That was so nice. I happily have the original picture. Albert was only 6 years old when he died.

I want to say one last thing. Although there were many controversies in Our Testa Family, I dearly loved them all and I love all of you, my children, nieces and nephews.

Albert Testa

Additional Photos

Gramma and Grampa Testa (Angelina and Michele) 1949

Gramma and Grampa Testa (Angelina and Michele) 1949

Catherine and Joseph Dispenziere
Gramma's mother and father

Giuseppe (Joseph) Testa
Grampa's father

Gertrude Testa as a baby

Gertrude and Catherine

Sisters Jo, Norma, Helen, Gertrude and Catherine

Teddy and friend as sailors

Gertrude, Dick and David Scott

Catherine and Frank Laratta Wedding

Helen and Nick Celfo

Norma and Doc DiOrio

Jo and Al Del Tufo

Mike and Marie Testa

Family from left Josephine, Norma, Grampa (Michele) Catherine, Gramma (Angelina), Helen, Teddy and Mike

Gramma (Angelina) looking outside her window

Mike in uniform

Teddy in uniform

www.ingramcontent.com/pod-product-compliance
Lightning Source LLC
Chambersburg PA
CBHW080450110426
42743CB00016B/3335